# Multiply on the Fly

by Suzanne Slade

illustrated by Erin E. Hunter

Numbers are an important part of our world. You can find them in school, sports, and nature. When you know how to multiply numbers, you can figure out almost anything!

Nine brilliant fireflies
twinkle in the dark—
glowing lights flash on and off.
How many in the park?

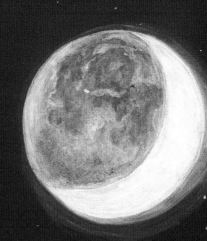

9 x 1 = ?

**Five lonely grasshoppers
sound their mating song.
Each strums two shiny wings.
How many play along?**

$$5 \times 2 = ?$$

Four lovely luna moths
rest upon a pine.
Each one spans three inches.
How long is the luna line?

4 x 3 =?

# 8 x 4 = ?

Eight daring dragonflies
soar into the sky.
Each is flapping four strong wings.
How many wings go by?

Six sturdy soldier ants
march around the yard.
Each uses five small eyes.
How many eyes stand guard?

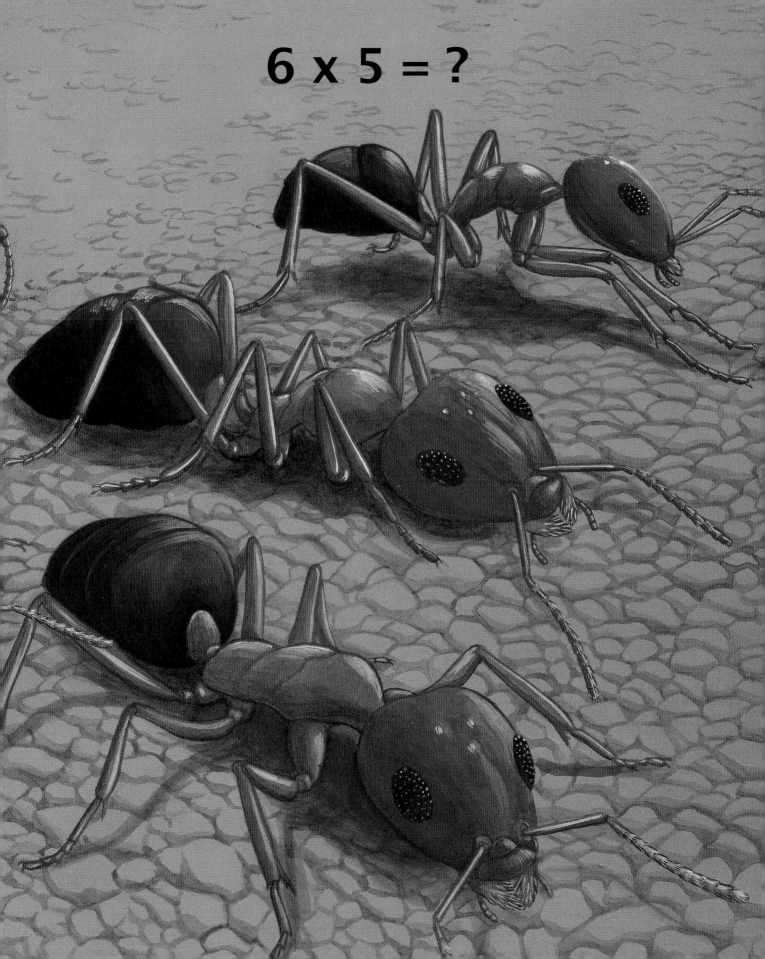

6 x 5 = ?

**Four hungry honey bees
dance a buggy beat—
tappin' with six furry legs.
How many dancing feet?**

$$4 \times 6 = ?$$

Eight little ladybugs,
wearing seven spots,
rest on fragrant flowers.
How many small black dots?

8 x 7 = ?

Three helpful pirate bugs
start their work at dawn.
Each eats eight spider mites.
How many pests are gone?

3 x 8 = ?

Seven stealthy walking sticks
climb onto a tree.
Each has nine long parts.
How many do you see?

7 x 9 = ?

Six swarms of butterflies
migrate in the fall.
Ten monarchs in each group,
how many fly in all?

# 6 x 10 = ?

Two silent spittlebugs
find a leafy home
and blow eleven bubbles.
How many in the foam?

2 x 11 = ?

# For Creative Minds

## Insect Body Parts

Insects don't have backbones as we do. They have a hard outer covering (called an exoskeleton) on the outside of their bodies.

Most insects have three pairs of legs for walking, swimming, and grabbing prey.

Many adult insects have two pairs of wings.

All bugs are insects, but not all insects are bugs.

Adult insects have three body parts: head, thorax, and abdomen.

The head holds the eyes, antennae, and mouthparts.

The thorax is right behind the head. Wings and legs attach to the thorax.

The abdomen is the back part of the insect and contains the heart and other major organs.

Most insects have one pair of antennae. Insects "wave" their antennae to sense what is around them by smell.

# Match the Insects

ant      honey bee      Monarch butterfly      dragonfly

firefly      long-horned grasshopper      ladybug      walking stick

1  These night fliers produce light to find mates. If too many outside lights are on, they have trouble finding each other.

2  To attract the ladies, these males create a mating call (some call a song). This species (and crickets) rub their two wings together to make their beautiful sound, while other species rub a wing against a leg.

3  These beetles eat up to 75 tasty aphids a day. Different kinds have different numbers of black spots on their wings.

4  These insects have four oval-shaped wings. They can fly up to 35 mph (56 kilometers per hour)! They can also hover in one place like a helicopter, or fly backwards.

5  Imagine having five eyes like this insect! They have two large compound eyes made of many lenses and three simple eyes. The simple eyes are on the forehead in a triangle.

6  These insects do special dances to let each other know where to find food. If flowers are near, they move in a circle. If flowers are far, they do a figure eight.

7  Their thin body parts look exactly like small twigs. When hungry enemies are near, these insects stay perfectly still.

8  To avoid the cold winters, these insects migrate. Some travel 3000 miles (4828 km) to find a warm place to stay during the cold winter.

Answers: 1. fireflies, 2. grasshoppers, 3. ladybugs, 4. dragonflies, 5. ants, 6. honey bees, 7. walking sticks, 8. Monarch butterflies

# Insect Life Cycles

Eggs hatch into larvae that don't look anything like the adults.

The larvae eat, grow, and molt. When they are grown, they turn into pupae.

The pupa stage is a time of change.

Adult insects emerge from pupae. Then they lay eggs to start the process all over again.

Names of insects and their larvae:

beetles, bees, wasps—grubs
butterflies, moths—caterpillars
mosquitoes—wrigglers or larvae
ants—larvae
flies—maggots

Amphibians (frogs, toads, and salamanders) also go through a complete metamorphosis. Larvae are called tadpoles or pollywogs.

egg

larva

## Complete Metamorphosis

adult

pupa (chrysalis or cocoon)

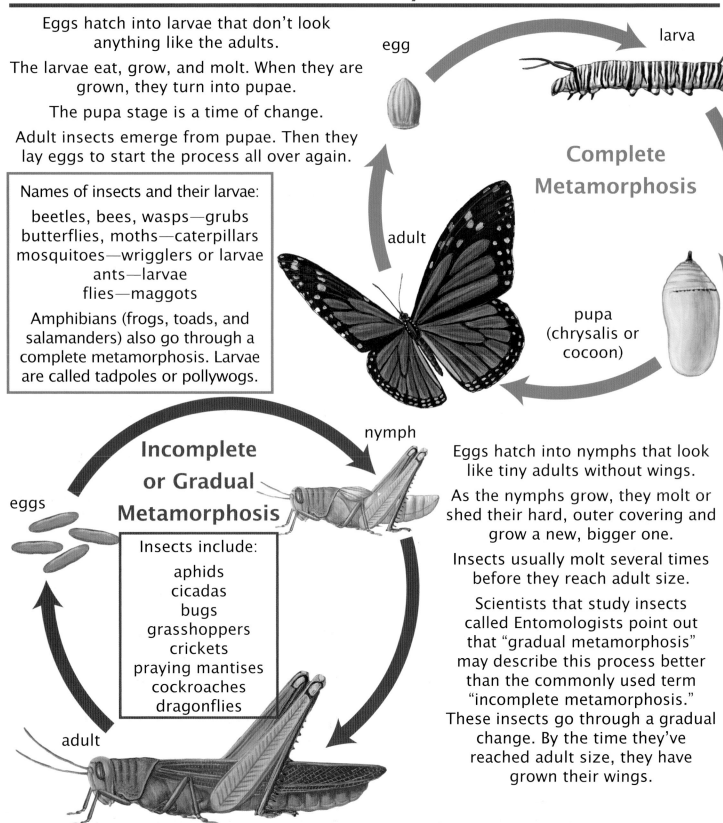

## Incomplete or Gradual Metamorphosis

nymph

eggs

adult

Insects include:

aphids
cicadas
bugs
grasshoppers
crickets
praying mantises
cockroaches
dragonflies

Eggs hatch into nymphs that look like tiny adults without wings.

As the nymphs grow, they molt or shed their hard, outer covering and grow a new, bigger one.

Insects usually molt several times before they reach adult size.

Scientists that study insects called Entomologists point out that "gradual metamorphosis" may describe this process better than the commonly used term "incomplete metamorphosis." These insects go through a gradual change. By the time they've reached adult size, they have grown their wings.

# Compare and Contrast

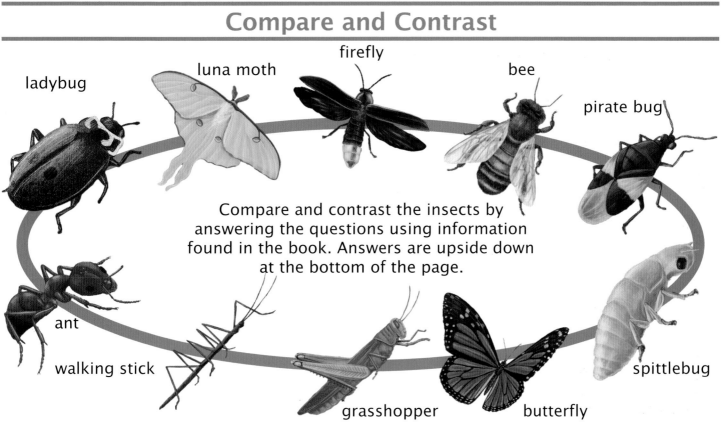

ladybug
luna moth
firefly
bee
pirate bug

Compare and contrast the insects by answering the questions using information found in the book. Answers are upside down at the bottom of the page.

ant
walking stick
grasshopper
butterfly
spittlebug

1 A ladybug is a type of beetle. What is the ladybug called when it hatches from its egg? Does it undergo complete or incomplete metamorphosis?

2 What is a cockroach called when it hatches from its egg? Does it undergo complete or incomplete metamorphosis?

3 What are some animals, other than insects, that undergo complete metamorphosis? To what animal group do they belong?

4 Ants undergo a complete metamorphosis. At what stage of life are the ants shown in this book?

5 Loud music or noise make it difficult for some insects to find mates. Bright outside lights make it difficult for which insect to find a mate?

6 Insect legs and wings (if they have wings) attach to what part of their body?

7 How do insects use their antennae? What part of our body do we use for that?

8 Insects are classified as "invertebrates" because they do not have backbones. What kind of skeleton do they have?

Answers: 1) grub/complete, 2) nymph/incomplete, 3) frogs, toads, and salamanders/amphibians, 4) adults, 5) fireflies, 6) thorax, 7) sense of smell/our noses, 8) insects have hard, outer coverings (exoskeletons)

# Multiplying Numbers

3 pirate bugs x 8 mites each = how many mites?

You could count
each mite to get
the answer.

Or, you could add
each group:

$8 + 8 + 8 = 24$

Or, you could
multiply:

$8 \times 3 = 24$

9 fireflies x 1 light each = how many lights? $9 \times 1 = ?$

5 grasshoppers x 2 wings each = how many wings? $2 + 2 + 2 + 2 + 2 = ?$ or $5 \times 2 = ?$

4 luna moths x 3 inches long = how many inches? $3 + 3 + 3 + 3 = ?$ or $4 \times 3 = ?$

8 dragonflies x 4 wings each = how many wings? $4 + 4 + 4 + 4 + 4 + 4 + 4 + 4 = ?$ or $8 \times 4 = ?$

6 ants x 5 eyes each = how many eyes? $5 + 5 + 5 + 5 + 5 + 5 = ?$ or $6 \times 5 = ?$

4 honey bees x 6 legs each = how many legs? $6 + 6 + 6 + 6 = ?$ or $4 \times 6 = ?$

8 ladybugs x 7 spots each = how many spots? $7 + 7 + 7 + 7 + 7 + 7 + 7 + 7 = ?$ or $8 \times 7 = ?$

7 walking sticks x 9 parts = how many parts? $9 + 9 + 9 + 9 + 9 + 9 + 9 = ?$ or $7 \times 9 = ?$

6 swarms of 10 butterflies = how many butterflies? $10 + 10 + 10 + 10 + 10 + 10 = ?$ or $6 \times 10 = ?$

2 spittlebugs x 11 bubbles = how many bubbles? $11 + 11 = ?$ or $2 \times 11 = ?$

# Insect Multiplication Table

It's best to memorize the basic multiplication facts. Until then, you can use a multiplication table to help find the answer. The top row and left-side column of numbers (in yellow) represent the numbers to be multiplied. To find the answer, run your finger over and down to where the row and column meet.

Do you think it matters which number is in the top row or first column?

Can you find any patterns in the numbers?

| x | 1 | 2 | 3 | 4 | 5 | 6 | 7 | 8 | 9 | 10 | 11 |
|---|---|---|---|---|---|---|---|---|---|----|----|
| 1 | 1 | 2 | 3 | 4 | 5 | 6 | 7 | 8 |   | 10 | 11 |
| 2 | 2 | 4 | 6 | 8 |   | 12 | 14 | 16 | 18 | 20 |   |
| 3 | 3 | 6 | 9 |   | 15 | 18 | 21 |   | 27 | 30 | 33 |
| 4 | 4 | 8 |   | 16 | 20 |   | 28 |   | 36 | 40 | 44 |
| 5 | 5 |   | 15 | 20 | 25 |   | 35 | 40 | 45 | 50 | 55 |
| 6 | 6 | 12 | 18 |   |   | 36 | 42 | 48 | 54 |   | 66 |
| 7 | 7 | 14 | 21 | 28 | 35 | 42 | 49 |   |   | 70 | 77 |
| 8 | 8 | 16 |   |   | 40 | 48 |   | 64 | 72 | 80 | 88 |
| 9 |   | 18 | 27 | 36 | 45 | 54 |   | 72 | 81 | 90 | 99 |
| 10 | 10 | 20 | 30 | 40 | 50 |   | 70 | 80 | 90 | 100 | 110 |
| 11 | 11 |   | 33 | 44 | 55 | 66 | 77 | 88 | 99 | 110 | 121 |

More multiplication activities are in the free online activities available on the book's homepage at www.SylvanDellPublishing.com.

Answers: 9 fireflies x 1 light each = 9 lights; 5 grasshoppers x 2 wings each = 10 wings; 4 luna moths x 3 inches long = 12 inches; 8 dragonflies x 4 wings each = 32 wings; 6 ants x 5 eyes each = 30 eyes; 4 honey bees x 6 legs each = 24 legs; 8 ladybugs x 7 spots each = 56 spots; 7 walking sticks x 9 parts = 63 parts; 6 swarms of 10 butterflies = 60 butterflies; 2 spittlebugs x 11 bubbles = 22 bubbles

With love to the best flyer I know, Brigadier General Fredric Buckingham (Ret), and his wife, Diane—SS
To Mom and Dad, who encouraged me to draw, and taught me to love nature (especially bugs)—EH
Thanks to the following people for verifying the accuracy of the insect information in this book:
· Dr. John Stoffolano, Professor, Department of Plant, Soil & Insect Sciences, University of Massachusetts, and Developer of the University's online Bug Net
· Faith Deering, Museum Educator, Historic Deerfield Museum
And thanks to Dr. Astrida Cirulis, Professor of Mathematics at Concordia University Chicago and President of Illinois Mathematics Teacher Educators, for reviewing the math-related information in the book.

Library of Congress Cataloging-in-Publication Data

Slade, Suzanne.
  Multiply on the fly / by Suzanne Slade ; illustrated by Erin E. Hunter.
    p. cm. --  (What's new at the zoo?) (What's the difference?)
  ISBN 978-1-60718-128-6 (hardcover) -- ISBN 978-1-60718-138-5 (softcover) -- ISBN 978-1-60718-148-4 (English ebook) -- ISBN 978-1-60718-158-3 (Spanish ebook)  1.  Multiplication--Juvenile literature. 2.  Insects--Juvenile literature.  I. Hunter, Erin E. ill. II. Title.
  QA115.S64 2011
  513.2'13--dc23
                              2011019886

Also available as eBooks featuring auto-flip, auto-read, 3D-page-curling, and selectable English and Spanish text and audio
Interest level: 004-009
Grade level: P-4
Lexile Level:  Lexile Code: AD
Curriculum keywords: compare/contrast, life cycle: metamorphosis, life cycles: animals, multiply/divide, classification (invertebrates)

Manufactured in China, June 2011
This product conforms to CPSIA 2008
First Printing
Published by Sylvan Dell Publishing
Mt. Pleasant, SC 29464